I0440914

Clean Cities 2012 Vehicle Buyer's Guide

The expanding availability of alternative fuels and advanced vehicles makes it easier than ever to reduce petroleum use, cut emissions, and save on fuel costs. This guide features a comprehensive list of vehicles set to hit the market in model year 2012.

Contents

Clean Cities
U.S. Department of Energy

Disclaimers

This report was prepared as an account of work sponsored by an agency of the United States government. Neither the United States government nor any agency thereof, nor any of their employees, makes any warranty, express or implied, or assumes any legal liability or responsibility for the accuracy, completeness, or usefulness of any information, apparatus, product, or process disclosed, or represents that its use would not infringe privately owned rights. Reference herein to any specific commercial product, process, or service by trade name, trademark, manufacturer, or otherwise does not necessarily constitute or imply its endorsement, recommendation, or favoring by the United States government or any agency thereof. The views and opinions of authors expressed herein do not necessarily state or reflect those of the United States government or any agency thereof.

The Clean Cities 2012 Vehicle Buyer's Guide and the information contained therein are not endorsed by Chrysler Group LLC.

Introduction

Photo from iStock/13111869

Drivers and fleet managers across the country are looking for ways to reduce petroleum use, fuel costs, and vehicle emissions. As you'll find in this guide, these goals are easier to achieve than ever before, with an expanding selection of vehicles that use gasoline or diesel more efficiently, or forego them altogether.

Plug-in electric vehicles made a grand entrance onto U.S. roadways in model year (MY) 2011, and their momentum in the market is poised for continued growth in 2012. Sales of the all-electric Nissan Leaf surpassed 8,000 in the fall of 2011, and the plug-in hybrid Chevy Volt is now available nationwide. Several new models from major automakers will become available throughout MY 2012, and drivers are benefitting from a rapidly growing network of charging stations, thanks to infrastructure development initiatives in many states.

Hybrid electric vehicles, which first entered the market just a decade ago, are ubiquitous today. Hybrid technology now allows drivers of all vehicle classes, from SUVs to luxury sedans to subcompacts, to slash fuel use and emissions.

Alternative fueling infrastructure is expanding in many regions, making natural gas, propane, ethanol, and biodiesel attractive and convenient choices for many consumers and fleets. And because fuel availability is the most important factor in choosing an alternative fuel vehicle, this growth opens up new possibilities for vehicle ownership.

About This Guide

This guide features model-specific information about vehicle specs, manufacturer suggested retail price (MSRP), fuel economy, and emissions. You can use this information to compare vehicles and help inform your buying decisions.

Fuel Economy

This guide includes city and highway fuel economy estimates from the U.S. Environmental Protection Agency (EPA). The estimates are based on laboratory tests conducted by manufacturers in accordance with federal regulations. EPA retests about 10% of vehicle models to confirm manufacturer results. Fuel economy estimates are also available on FuelEconomy.gov. For some newer vehicle models, EPA data was not available at the time of this guide's publication; in these cases, manufacturer estimates are provided, if available.

EPA Smog Scores

Smog scores reflect vehicle tailpipe emissions that contribute to local and regional air quality problems, such as smog, haze, and related health issues, as determined by EPA. Scores range from 0 to 10, where 10 is cleanest.

Photo from iStock/12473993

Greenhouse Gas Emissions Scores

Greenhouse gas (GHG) emissions scores reflect tailpipe emissions of carbon dioxide and other GHGs, which impact the planet's climate. Scores range from 0 to 10, where 10 is best. The GHG scores in this guide do not reflect emissions related to the production or distribution of fuels or vehicles.

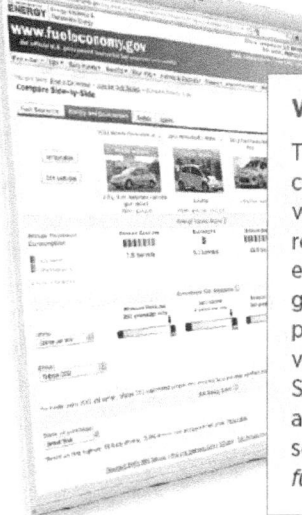

What's Your Energy Impact?

The United States imports about half the petroleum it consumes. By choosing alternative fuel vehicles and vehicles with high fuel efficiency, we can reduce U.S. reliance on imported petroleum and strengthen U.S. energy security. The Find A Car tool on FuelEconomy. gov allows consumers and fleet managers to compare the energy impacts of new and used light-duty vehicle models. The tool features an Energy Impact Score that reveals the number of barrels of petroleum a vehicle will likely consume each year from domestic sources and from imports. Explore the tool at *www. fueleconomy.gov/feg/findacar.shtml#findacar.*

Compressed Natural Gas

Honda Civic Natural Gas

- 1.8L 4 cyl engine
- Starting MSRP: $25,490
- 24 miles per gallon of gasoline-equivalent (mpge) city, 36 mpge highway
- Emissions data not available

Courtesy of American Honda Motor Co. Inc.

Compressed natural gas vehicles have low fuel costs.

Compressed natural gas (CNG) vehicles are powered by the same fuel used for cooking and heating in many homes. Domestic natural gas supplies are plentiful, and some producers even capture renewable natural gas from landfills and sewage treatment facilities. CNG is usually less expensive than gasoline, and the savings can help offset the purchase price of a CNG vehicle.

In 2012, two dedicated natural gas vehicles are available directly from major manufacturers: the natural gas Chevrolet Express/GMC Savana and the Honda Civic Natural Gas. These vehicles are available through authorized dealerships.

Ford offers several of its light- and medium-duty vans and trucks with CNG/propane prep packages (see page 9 for a list of models). A qualified system retrofitter can convert these vehicles to run on CNG. Ford provides calibration guidance to retrofitters so that converted vehicles maintain their factory engine warranties.

In general, new and used conventional vehicles can be converted to run on CNG at a cost of about $8,000 to $12,000 per

GMC Savana 2500. Photo from General Motors

Chevrolet Express 2500/3500
GMC Savana 2500/3500

- 6.0L 8 cyl engine
- Starting MSRP: $43,000
- Fuel economy and emissions data not available

vehicle. Learn more about conversions in the box below. CNG vehicles, including some conversions, may be eligible for a federal tax credit or state incentive (see page 29).

Fuel availability may be the deciding factor.

If you are considering the purchase of a CNG vehicle or converting a conventional vehicle to run on CNG, it's important to first determine whether you have access to CNG fueling infrastructure. In December 2011, there were more than 900 CNG fueling stations across the country. See page 23 for information about finding stations in your area.

VPG MV-1

- 4.6L 8 cyl engine
- Starting MSRP: $39,950
- 11 mpge city, 16 mpge highway
- Smog Score: 8
- GHG Score: 2

Photo from the Vehicle Production Group

Converting Vehicles to Run on Alternative Fuels

An increasing number of alternative and advanced vehicles are available from major manufacturers, but vehicle conversions provide additional options. Many conventional vehicles can be converted to run on natural gas, propane, electricity, or other alternative fuels. All conversions must meet emissions and safety standards instituted by EPA, the National Highway Traffic Safety Administration, and all relevant state agencies. Conversions must be performed by an authorized technician associated with a manufacturer that holds all relevant emissions-related certifications and tampering exemptions. Find out more at *www.afdc.energy.gov/afdc/ vehicles/conversions.html*.

Photo from iStock/ 13079147

Propane

Chevrolet Express 3500/4500
GMC Savana 3500/4500

- 6.0L 8 cyl engine
- Starting MSRP: $46,390
- Fuel economy and emissions data not available

Chevrolet Express Cutaway Van with RV Upfit application.
Photo from General Motors

Propane is widely available.

Propane is a clean-burning fuel that's been used in transportation for decades. Also known as liquefied petroleum gas (LPG), propane is the most commonly used alternative motor fuel in the world. Propane typically costs about one-third less than gasoline. See page 23 for information about finding propane fueling stations in your area.

Choose your path to propane.

In 2012, General Motors is offering dedicated LPG options for the Chevrolet Express and GMC Savana 3500 and 4500 cutaway vans equipped with 6.0L V-8 engines. These vans are covered by GM's three-year, 36,000-mile new vehicle limited warranty and five-year, 100,000-mile limited powertrain warranty and vehicle emissions warranty, meeting all EPA and California Air Resources Board (CARB) emissions certification requirements. These vehicles can be ordered directly through a GM dealership.

The following 2012 Ford vehicles are available with dedicated LPG fuel systems and can be ordered directly through an authorized Ford dealership:

- Roush/Ford F-250 and F-350 Super Duty Pickups (6.2L V-8)
- Roush/Ford F-450 and F-550 Chassis Cab (6.8L V-10)
- Roush/Ford E-150, E-250, and E-350 Cargo and Passenger Vans (5.4L V-8)
- Roush/Ford E-450 Cutaway (6.8L V-10)

Ford E-350 Van. *Photo from Ford Motor Co.*

Ford also offers the following light- and medium-duty vans and trucks with CNG/ LPG prep packages. A qualified system retrofitter can convert these vehicles to run on LPG.

- Ford E-150, E-250, and E-350 Cargo and Passenger Vans (5.4L V-8)
- Ford F-250 and F-350 Super Duty Pickups (6.2L V-8)
- Ford Transit Connect (2.0L 4 cylinder)

Ford Super Duty F-250. *Photo from Ford Motor Co.*

Several qualified system retrofitters can convert a variety of late-model gasoline vehicles to propane operation. Conversion has little effect on horsepower, torque, towing capacity, or factory warranty. Learn more about conversions on page 7.

A federal tax credit may be available to reduce the differential cost of a propane vehicle, including some conversions (see page 29).

Get More Information About Alternative Fuels and Advanced Vehicles

Clean Cities' Alternative Fuels and Advanced Vehicles Data Center (AFDC) provides information, data, and tools to help fleet managers and other transportation decision makers find ways to reduce petroleum use. Learn more about the properties of biodiesel. Broaden your understanding of electric-drive vehicle technologies. Build a business case for natural gas fueling infrastructure. It's all online at *www.afdc.energy.gov.*

All-Electric Vehicles

Mitusbishi i

- 66 kW electric motor
- Starting MSRP: $29,125
- All-electric range: 62 miles
- 126 mpge city,
  99 mpge highway
- Smog Score: 10
- GHG score: 10

Photo from Mitsubishi Motor Co.

All-electric vehicles have zero tailpipe emissions.

All-electric vehicles (EVs) use batteries to store the electrical energy that powers the motor. EV batteries are charged by plugging into an electric power source. They can also be charged in part by regenerative braking, which generates electricity from some of the energy normally lost when braking. Although electric power plants may contribute to air pollution, EPA classifies EVs as zero-emission vehicles, because their motors produce no exhaust.

Currently available EVs can travel 60 to 100 miles on a single charge, depending on the model. According to the U.S. Department of Transportation Federal Highway Administration, 100 miles is a sufficient range for more than 90% of all household vehicle trips in the United States. And EV drivers are now benefitting from a growing network of public charging stations. See page 23 for information about finding public stations in your area.

EVs are more expensive than similar conventional and hybrid electric vehicles, but some costs may be recovered through fuel savings, a tax credit, or state incentives. See page 29 for more information.

Coda

- 100kW electric motor
- Starting MSRP: $39,900
- All-electric range: 150 miles
  (manufacturer estimate)
- Fuel economy and emissions
  data not available

Photo from Coda Automotive

Ford Focus Electric

- 105 kW electric motor
- Starting MSRP: $39,200
- All-electric range: 100 miles (manufacturer estimate)
- Fuel economy data not available
- Smog Score: 10
- GHG Score: 10

Photo from Ford Motor Co.

Azure Dynamics/Ford Transit Connect

- 52 kW electric motor
- Starting MSRP: Not available
- All-electric range: 56 miles
- 62 mpge city, 62 mpge highway
- Smog Score: 10
- GHG Score: 10

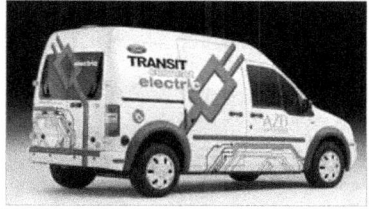

Photo from Ford Motor Co.

Plug-In Vehicles and EPA Labels

EPA labels for all-electric vehicles (EVs) display fuel economy estimates expressed in *kilowatt-hours per 100 miles* and in *miles per gallon of gasoline-equivalent (mpge)*. Mpge represents the number of miles a vehicle can travel using a quantity of fuel with the same energy content as a gallon of gasoline. For plug-in hybrid electric vehicles (PHEVs), EPA labels display separate fuel economy estimates for electric-only and gasoline-only modes. Estimates for gasoline-only operation are expressed in *miles per gallon* and in *gallons per 100 miles*. All this information allows for comparisons across different types of vehicles and fuels. For more information, visit *www.fueleconomy.gov/feg/label*.

EPA plug-in vehicle labels also contain information about GHG emissions and air pollution. This information reflects tailpipe emissions only. It does not account for emissions associated with the production of electricity, gasoline, or any other fuel that powers the vehicle. For information about well-to-wheel emissions of conventional and plug-in vehicles, visit *www.afdc.energy.gov/afdc/vehicles/electric_emissions.php*.

Honda Fit EV

- Starting MSRP: $36,625
- All-electric range: 100 miles (manufacturer estimate)
- Vehicle specs, fuel economy, and emissions data not available

Courtesy of American Honda Motor Co. Inc.

Nissan Leaf

- 80 kW electric motor
- Starting MSRP: $35,200
- All-electric range: 73 miles
- 106 mpge city, 92 mpge highway
- Smog Score: 10
- GHG Score: 10

©2011 Nissan

Tesla Model S

- Starting MSRP: $50,000
- All-electric range: 300 miles (manufacturer estimate)
- Fuel economy, vehicle specs, and emissions data not available

Photo from Tesla Motors

Toyota RAV4 EV

- MSRP, vehicle specs, fuel economy, and emissions data not available

Photo from Toyota Motor Corp.

Wheego LiFe

- 15 kW electric motor
- Starting MSRP: $32,995
- All-electric range: 100 miles (manufacturer estimate)
- Fuel economy data not available
- Smog Score: 10
- GHG Score: 10

Photo from Wheego Electric Cars

Plug-In Hybrid Electric Vehicles

Chevrolet Volt

- 1.4L 4 cyl engine
- 111 kW electric motor
- Starting MSRP: $40,280
- All-electric range: 35 miles
- 95 mpge city, 93 mpge highway (electricity only)
- 35 mpg city, 40 mpg highway (gasoline only)
- Smog Score: 10 (electricity), 6 (gasoline)
- GHG Score: 10 (electricity), 8 (gasoline)

Photo from General Motors

Plug-in hybrids can run on gasoline or electricity.

Plug-in hybrid electric vehicles (PHEVs) use batteries to power an electric motor and use another fuel, such as gasoline or diesel, to power an internal combustion engine. Powering the vehicle some of the time with electricity from the grid cuts petroleum consumption and tailpipe emissions, relative to conventional vehicles. When running on gasoline, PHEVs, like hybrid electric vehicles, consume less fuel and produce lower emissions than comparable conventional vehicles. PHEVs are sometimes called extended range electric vehicles.

PHEV batteries can be charged by plugging into an outside electric power source, by the internal combustion engine, and through regenerative braking. But PHEVs don't have to be plugged in before driving. They can be fueled solely with gasoline, like a conventional hybrid, but they will not achieve maximum fuel economy or take advantage of their all-electric capabilities without charging.

Photo from Toyota Motor Corp.

Toyota Prius Plug-In Hybrid

- 1.8L 4 cyl engine
- 60 kW electric motor
- Starting MSRP: $32,000
- All-electric range: 15 miles (manufacturer estimate)
- Fuel economy and emissions data not available

Hybrid Electric Vehicles

Ford Fusion Hybrid

- 2.5L 4 cyl engine
- Starting MSRP: $28,600
- 41 mpg city,
  36 mpg highway
- Smog Score: 7
- GHG Score: 9

Photo from Ford Motor Co.

Hybrids save fuel and cut emissions.

Hybrid electric vehicles (HEVs) are powered by an internal combustion engine and an electric motor that uses energy stored in a battery. HEVs run on gasoline or an alternative fuel and don't need to be plugged in to recharge the battery. The extra power provided by the electric motor allows for a smaller engine, resulting in better fuel economy without sacrificing performance.

Some HEVs achieve fuel economy ratings of 40 to 50 mpg. And they produce lower levels of air pollutants and GHG emissions than conventional vehicles.

Hybrid configuration affects performance and price.

HEVs range from mild to full hybrids. Full hybrids can run on battery power alone at idle and low speeds. When speeds increase, the electric motor works with the gasoline engine to provide power. Full hybrids are 25% to 40% more fuel efficient than comparable conventional vehicles.

Mild hybrids use a battery and electric motor to help power the vehicle. This allows the engine to shut off when the vehicle stops at traffic signals and in stop-and-go traffic, thus improving fuel economy. Mild hybrids cannot power the vehicle using electricity alone. These vehicles cost less than full hybrids, but they provide more modest increases in fuel economy.

Photo from Kia Motors America

Kia Optima

- 2.4L 4 cyl engine
- Starting MSRP: $26,500
- 35 mpg city, 40 mpg highway
- Smog Score: 8
- GHG Score: 8

BMW ActiveHybrid 5

- 3.0L 6 cyl engine
- Starting MSRP: $88,900
- Fuel economy and emissions data not available

Photo from BMW of North America

BMW ActiveHybrid 7

- 4.4L 8 cyl engine
- Starting MSRP: $97,000
- 17 mpg city, 24 mpg highway
- Smog Score: 5
- GHG Score: 4

BMW ActiveHybrid 7L

- 4.4L 8 cyl engine
- Starting MSRP: $101,000
- 17 mpg city, 24 mpg highway
- Smog Score: 5
- GHG Score: 4

Buick Regal Hybrid

- 2.4L 4 cyl engine
- Starting MSRP: $26,670
- 25 mpg city, 36 mpg highway
- Emissions data not available

Photo from General Motors

Buick LaCrosse Hybrid

- 2.4L 4 cyl engine
- Starting MSRP: $30,820
- 25 mpg city, 36 mpg highway
- Smog Score: 6
- GHG Score: 7

Cadillac Escalade Hybrid

- 6.0L 8 cyl engine
- Starting MSRP: $74,135
- 20 mpg city, 23 mpg highway
- Smog Score: 5
- GHG Score: 4

Chevrolet Silverado 1500 Hybrid 2WD/4WD
GMC Sierra 1500 Hybrid 2WD/4WD

- 6.0L 8 cyl engine
- Starting MSRP: $38,725
- 20 mpg city, 23 mpg highway
- Smog Score: 5
- GHG Score: 4

Chevrolet Silverado 1500 Hybrid.
Photo from General Motors

Chevrolet Tahoe 1500 Hybrid 2WD/4WD
GMC Yukon 1500 Hybrid 2WD/4WD

- 6.0L 8 cyl engine
- Starting MSRP: $58,145
- 20 mpg city, 23 mpg highway
- Smog Score: 5
- GHG Score: 4

Ford Escape Hybrid FWD/4WD

- 2.5L 4 cyl engine
- Starting MSRP: $30,570
- 34 mpg city, 31 mpg highway
- Smog Score: 7
- GHG Score: 7

Honda Civic Hybrid

- 1.5L 4 cyl engine
- Starting MSRP: $24,050
- 44 mpg city, 44 mpg highway
- Smog Score: 8
- GHG Score: 9

Courtesy of American Honda Motor Co. Inc.

Honda CR-Z

- 1.5L 4 cyl engine
- Starting MSRP: $19,345
- 31 mpg city, 37 mpg highway
- Smog Score: 8
- GHG Score: 8

Honda Insight

- 1.3L 4 cyl engine
- Starting MSRP: $18,200
- 40 mpg city, 43 mpg highway
- Smog Score: 8
- GHG Score: 9

Hyundai Sonata Hybrid

- 2.4L 4 cyl engine
- Starting MSRP: $25,795
- 35 mpg city, 40 mpg highway
- Smog Score: 8
- GHG Score: 8

Photo from Hyundai Motor America

Infiniti M35h Hybrid

- 3.5L 6 cyl engine
- Starting MSRP: $53,700
- 27 mpg city, 32 mpg highway
- Smog Score: 5
- GHG Score: 7

©2011 Nissan

Lexus CT 200h

- 1.8L 4 cyl engine
- Starting MSRP: $29,120
- 43 mpg city, 40 mpg highway
- Smog Score: 7
- GHG Score: 9

Photo from Toyota Motor Corp.

Lexus GS 450h

- 3.5L 6 cyl engine
- Starting MSRP: $58,950
- 22 mpg city, 25 mpg highway
- Smog Score: 7
- GHG Score: 5

Lexus HS 250h

- 2.5L 4 cyl engine
- Starting MSRP: $36,330
- 35 mpg city, 34 mpg highway
- Smog Score: 7
- GHG Score: 8

Lexus LS 600h L

- 5.0L 8 cyl engine
- Starting MSRP: $112,250
- 19 mpg city, 23 mpg highway
- Smog Score: 7
- GHG Score: 4

Lexus RX 450h AWD

- 3.5L 6 cyl engine
- Starting MSRP: $45,235
- 30 mpg city, 28 mpg highway
- Smog Score: 7
- GHG Score: 7

Hydrogen Fuel Cell Vehicles

A hydrogen fuel cell vehicle combines hydrogen gas with oxygen from the air to produce electricity, which drives an electric motor. Because these vehicles are powered by hydrogen, they produce no harmful tailpipe emissions. Several challenges must be overcome before these vehicles can be commercially available, but some manufacturers produce them in very limited numbers, including the following models:

- Honda FCX Clarity
- Mercedes-Benz F-Cell

Honda FCX Clarity. Courtesy of American Honda Motor Co. Inc.

Lincoln MKZ Hybrid

- 2.5L 4 cyl engine
- Starting MSRP: $34,649
- 41 mpg city, 36 mpg highway
- Smog Score: 7
- GHG Score: 9

Photo from Ford Motor Co.

Mercedes-Benz S400 Hybrid

- 3.5L 6 cyl engine
- Starting MSRP: $91,850
- 19 mpg city, 25 mpg highway
- Smog Score: 6
- GHG Score: 4

Photo from Mercedes-Benz USA

Porsche Panamera S Hybrid

- 3.0L 6 cyl engine
- Starting MSRP: $95,000
- 22 mpg city, 30 mpg highway
- Smog Score: 5
- GHG Score: 6

Photo from Porsche Cars North America

Porsche Cayenne S Hybrid

- 3.0L 6 cyl engine
- Starting MSRP: $67,700
- 20 mpg city, 24 mpg highway
- Smog Score: 6
- GHG Score: 4

Toyota Camry Hybrid

- 2.4L 4 cyl engine
- Starting MSRP: $27,050
- 31 mpg city, 35 mpg highway
- Smog Score: 9
- GHG Score: 8

Toyota Highlander AWD Hybrid

- 3.5L 6 cyl engine
- Starting MSRP: $38,120
- 28 mpg city, 28 mpg highway
- Smog Score: 8
- GHG Score: 7

Toyota Prius Hybrid

- 1.8L 4 cyl engine
- Starting MSRP: $23,520
- 51 mpg city, 48 mpg highway
- Smog Score: 7
- GHG Score: 10

Toyota Prius *v*

- 1.8L 4 cyl engine
- Starting MSRP: $26,400
- 44 mpg city, 40 mpg highway
- Smog Score: 7
- GHG Score: 9

Photo from Toyota Motor Corp.

Volkswagen Touareg Hybrid

- 3.0L 6 cyl engine
- Starting MSRP: $61,110
- 20 mpg city, 24 mpg highway
- Smog Score: 6
- GHG Score: 4

Photo from Volkswagen Group of America

ıd Emissions

art of its true cost. Use
determine total lifetime
ownership costs, including fuel use and maintenance. The easy-to-use online tool, available at *www.afdc.energy.gov/calculator*, compares the thousands of vehicles on the market today. It also allows users to evaluate a vehicle's emissions benefits, providing side-by-side comparisons of models that use conventional fuels, alternative fuels, and electricity.

To stay updated on the prices of alternative fuels and how they compare to gasoline prices, see the Clean Cities Alternative Fuel Price Report, available online at *www.afdc.energy.gov/afdc/price_report.html*.

Ethanol Flex-Fuel Vehicles

Dodge Charger

- 3.6L 6 cyl engine
- Starting MSRP: $25,495
- 13 mpg city, 19 mpg highway (E85)
- 18 mpg city, 27 mpg highway (gasoline)
- Smog Score: 5 (E85), 5 (gasoline)
- GHG Score: 4 (E85), 4 (gasoline)

Photo from Chrysler Group LLC

Flex-fuel vehicles can operate on gasoline or E85.

E85 is a blend of gasoline and ethanol. E85's ethanol content ranges between 51% and 83%, depending on geographical location and season.* Flex-fuel vehicles (FFVs) are able to run on gasoline, E85, or any combination of the two. According to EPA estimates, the fuel economy of today's FFVs is 20% to 25% lower when running on E85, because ethanol contains less energy per gallon than gasoline. The price of E85, however, can be lower than gasoline, offsetting the loss in fuel economy. An FFV is often distinguished by a logo on the back of the vehicle, and many FFVs have yellow fuel caps.

Today, E85 is available at more than 2,400 locations. See page 23 for information about finding E85 stations near you.

* *The E85 fuel economy estimates presented in this section are based on tests with blends containing 85% ethanol.*

Bentley Continental GT

- 6.0L 12 cyl engine
- Starting MSRP: $189,900
- 8 mpg city, 12 mpg highway (E85)
- 14 mpg city, 19 mpg highway (gasoline)
- Smog Score: 5 (E85), 5 (gasoline)
- GHG Score: 1 (E85), 1 (gasoline)

Bentley Continental Supersports

- 6.0L 12 cyl engine
- Starting MSRP: $267,200
- 8 mpg city, 12 mpg highway (E85)
- 14 mpg city, 19 mpg highway (gasoline)
- Smog Score: 5 (E85), 5 (gasoline)
- GHG Score: 1 (E85), 1 (gasoline)

Bentley Continental Flying Spur

- 6.0L 12 cyl engine
- Starting MSRP: $181,200
- 8 mpg city, 11 mpg highway (E85)
- 13 mpg city, 19 mpg highway (gasoline)
- Smog Score: 5 (E85), 5 (gasoline)
- GHG Score: 1 (E85), 1 (gasoline)

Photo from Bentley Motors Limited

Buick LaCrosse FWD/AWD

- 3.6L 6 cyl engine
- Starting MSRP: $32,440
- 13 mpg city, 19 mpg highway (E85)
- 17 mpg city, 27 mpg highway (gasoline)
- Smog Score: 6 (E85), 6 (gasoline)
- GHG Score: 4 (E85), 5 (gasoline)

Photo from General Motors

Buick Regal

- 2.4L 4 cyl engine
- Starting MSRP: $26,670
- 15 mpg city, 22 mpg highway (E85)
- 19 mpg city, 31 mpg highway (gasoline)
- Smog Score: 6 (E85), 6 (gasoline)
- GHG Score: 5 (E85), 5 (gasoline)

Buick Regal Turbo

- 2.0L 4 cyl engine
- Starting MSRP: $30,735
- 13 mpg city, 22 mpg highway (E85)
- 18 mpg city, 29 mpg highway (gasoline)
- Smog Score: 6 (E85), 6 (gasoline)
- GHG Score: 5 (E85), 5 (gasoline)

Cadillac Escalade ESV 2WD/AWD

- 6.2L 8 cyl engine
- Starting MSRP: $66,080
- 10 mpg city, 15 mpg highway (E85)
- 14 mpg city, 18 mpg highway (gasoline)
- Smog Score: 5 (E85), 5 (gasoline)
- GHG Score: 2 (E85), 1 (gasoline)

Photo from General Motors

Cadillac Escalade 2WD/AWD

- 6.2L 8 cyl engine
- Starting MSRP: $63,455
- 10 mpg city, 15 mpg highway (E85)
- 14 mpg city, 18 mpg highway (gasoline)
- Smog Score: 5 (E85), 5 (gasoline)
- GHG Score: 2 (E85), 1 (gasoline)

Cadillac Escalade EXT AWD

- 6.2L 8 cyl engine
- Starting MSRP: $62,160
- 9 mpg city, 13 mpg highway (E85)
- 13 mpg city, 18 mpg highway (gasoline)
- Smog Score: 5 (E85), 5 (gasoline)
- GHG Score: 1 (E85), 1 (gasoline)

Cadillac SRX 2WD/AWD

- 3.6L 6 cyl engine
- Starting MSRP: $36,060
- 12 mpg city, 18 mpg highway (E85)
- 17 mpg city, 24 mpg highway (gasoline)
- Smog Score: 6 (E85), 6 (gasoline)
- GHG Score: 4 (E85), 3 (gasoline)

Photo from General Motors

Chevrolet Avalanche 1500 2WD/4WD

- 5.3L 8 cyl engine
- Starting MSRP: $36,300
- 11 mpg city, 16 mpg highway (E85)
- 15 mpg city, 21 mpg highway (gasoline)
- Smog Score: 5 (E85), 5 (gasoline)
- GHG Score: 3 (E85), 2 (gasoline)

Chevrolet Caprice Police Petrol Vehicle

- 3.6L 6 cyl engine
- Starting MSRP: Not available
- 13 mpg city, 18 mpg highway (E85)
- 18 mpg city, 26 mpg highway (gasoline)
- Smog Score: 6 (E85), 6 (gasoline)
- GHG Score: 4 (E85), 4 (gasoline)

Chevrolet Equinox FWD/AWD

- 2.4L 4 cyl engine
- Starting MSRP: $23,450
- 15 mpg city, 22 mpg highway (E85)
- 22 mpg city, 32 mpg highway (gasoline)
- Smog Score: 6 (E85), 6 (gasoline)
- GHG Score: 6 (E85), 6 (gasoline)

Photo from General Motors

Chevrolet Equinox FWD/AWD

- 3.0L 6 cyl engine
- Starting MSRP: $27,675
- 12 mpg city, 18 mpg highway (E85)
- 17 mpg city, 24 mpg highway (gasoline)
- Smog Score: 6 (E85), 6 (gasoline)
- GHG Score: 4 (E85), 3 (gasoline)

Chevrolet Express 1500 2WD/AWD GMC Savana G1500 2WD/AWD

- 5.3L 8 cyl engine
- Starting MSRP: $30,035
- 10 mpg city, 13 mpg highway (E85)
- 13 mpg city, 18 mpg highway (gasoline)
- Smog Score: 6 (E85), 6 (gasoline)
- GHG Score: 1 (E85), 1 (gasoline)

Chevrolet Express 2500/3500 GMC Savana 2500/3500

- 4.8L 8 cyl engine
- Starting MSRP: $28,825
- 8 mpg city, 11 mpg highway (E85)
- 12 mpg city, 17 mpg highway (gasoline)
- Smog Score: 2 (E85), 2 (gasoline)
- GHG Score: 1 (E85), 1 (gasoline)

Chevrolet Express 2500/3500 GMC Savana 2500/3500

- 6.0L 8 cyl engine
- Starting MSRP: $29,820
- 8 mpg city, 11 mpg highway (E85)
- 11 mpg city, 16 mpg highway (gasoline)
- Smog Score: 2 (E85), 2 (gasoline)
- GHG Score: 1 (E85), 1 (gasoline)

Find an Alternative Fuel Station or Electric Charging Station

Thousands of fueling sites across the country provide alternatives to gasoline and diesel fuel. The AFDC's Alternative Fueling Station Locator (*www.afdc.energy.gov/stations*) helps drivers navigate to stations that provide propane, biodiesel, natural gas, electric charging, and E85. Users can also download the data into a spreadsheet. There's even a mobile version at *www.afdc.energy.gov/stations/m.*

Photo from Charles Bensinger, Renewable Energy Partners of New Mexico, NREL/PIX 13531

Chevrolet Impala

- 3.6L 6 cyl engine
- Starting MSRP: $25,645
- 13 mpg city, 22 mpg highway (E85)
- 18 mpg city, 30 mpg highway (gasoline)
- Smog Score: 6 (E85), 6 (gasoline)
- GHG Score: 4 (E85), 4 (gasoline)

Chevrolet Impala Police Package

- 3.6L 6 cyl engine
- Starting MSRP, fuel economy, and emissions data not available

Chevrolet Malibu

- 2.4L 4 cyl engine
- Starting MSRP: $22,085 Fleet only
- 15 mpg city, 23 mpg highway (E85)
- 22 mpg city, 33 mpg highway (gasoline)
- Smog Score: 6 (E85), 6 (gasoline)
- GHG Score: 6 (E85), 6 (gasoline)

Photo from General Motors

Chevrolet Silverado 1500 2WD/4WD
GMC Sierra 1500 2WD/4WD

- 4.8L 8 cyl engine
- Starting MSRP: $23,275
- 10 mpg city, 14 mpg highway (E85)
- 14 mpg city, 19 mpg highway (gasoline)
- Smog Score: 5 (E85), 5 (gasoline)
- GHG Score: 2 (E85), 1 (gasoline)

GMC Sierra 1500. Photo from General Motors

Improve Your Fuel Economy

Driving behaviors significantly impact fuel economy. To get the most out of each gallon (or kilowatt-hour), follow these tips:

- **Drive sensibly:** Avoid jack-rabbit starts, aggressive braking, and swift acceleration.
- **Don't speed:** Fuel economy decreases at speeds above 60 mph due to wind resistance.
- **Remove excess weight:** Don't keep unnecessary items in your vehicle.
- **Remove rooftop boxes and racks when not in use:** Increased drag lowers fuel economy.
- **Avoid idling:** Turn off your engine when parked.
- **Keep tires inflated:** Check the sticker inside your door or glove box for the proper pressure.
- **Keep the engine tuned:** Delaying maintenance can impact fuel efficiency.
- **Combine trips:** Several short trips from cold starts use more fuel than one multipurpose trip.

For more tips and information, visit *www.fueleconomy.gov/feg/drive.shtml*.

Photo from iStock/15335450

Chevrolet Silverado 1500
GMC Sierra 1500 2WD/4WD

- 5.3L 8 cyl engine
- Starting MSRP: $23,975
- 11 mpg city, 16 mpg highway (E85)
- 15 mpg city, 21 mpg highway (gasoline)
- Smog Score: 5 (E85), 5 (gasoline)
- GHG Score: 3 (E85), 2 (gasoline)

Chevrolet Silverado 1500
GMC Sierra 1500 2WD/4WD

- 6.2L 8 cyl engine
- Starting MSRP: $33,525
- 9 mpg city, 13 mpg highway (E85)
- 13 mpg city, 18 mpg highway (gasoline)
- Smog Score: 5 (E85), 5 (gasoline)
- GHG Score: 1 (E85), 1 (gasoline)

Chevrolet Suburban C1500
GMC Yukon C1500 2WD/4WD

- 5.3L 8 cyl engine
- Starting MSRP: $41,730
- 11 mpg city, 16 mpg highway (E85)
- 15 mpg city, 21 mpg highway (gasoline)
- Smog Score: 5 (E85), 5 (gasoline)
- GHG Score: 3 (E85), 2 (gasoline)

Chevrolet Tahoe 1500
GMC Yukon 1500 2WD/4WD

- 5.3L 8 cyl engine
- Starting MSRP: $37,980
- 11 mpg city, 16 mpg highway (E85)
- 15 mpg city, 21 mpg highway (gasoline)
- Smog Score: 5 (E85), 5 (gasoline)
- GHG Score: 3 (E85), 2 (gasoline)

Chevrolet Tahoe Police Package

- 5.3L 8 cyl engine
- Starting MSRP, fuel economy, and emissions data not available

Chrysler 200 S

- 3.6L 6 cyl engine
- Starting MSRP: $26,365
- 14 mpg city, 21 mpg highway (E85)
- 19 mpg city, 29 mpg highway (gasoline)
- Smog Score: 6 (E85), 6 (gasoline)
- GHG Score: 5 (E85), 5 (gasoline)

Chrysler 300

- 3.6L 6 cyl engine
- Starting MSRP: $27,170
- 13 mpg city, 19 mpg highway (E85)
- 18 mpg city, 27 mpg highway (gasoline)
- Smog Score: 5 (E85), 5 (gasoline)
- GHG Score: 4 (E85), 4 (gasoline)

Chrysler Town & Country

- 3.6L 6 cyl engine
- Starting MSRP: $29,995
- 12 mpg city, 18 mpg highway (E85)
- 17 mpg city, 25 mpg highway (gasoline)
- Smog Score: 6 (E85), 6 (gasoline)
- GHG Score: 4 (E85), 4 (gasoline)

Photo from Chrysler Group LLC

Dodge Avenger

- 3.6L 6 cyl engine
- Starting MSRP: $23,995
- 14 mpg city, 21 mpg highway (E85)
- 19 mpg city, 29 mpg highway (gasoline)
- Smog Score: 6 (E85), 6 (gasoline)
- GHG Score: 5 (E85), 5 (gasoline)

Dodge Charger Police Pursuit

- 3.6L 6 cyl engine
- Starting MSRP, fuel economy, and
  emissions data not available

Dodge Durango 2WD/4WD

- 3.6L 6 cyl engine
- Starting MSRP: $28,995
- 12 mpg city, 17 mpg highway (E85)
- 16 mpg city, 23 mpg highway (gasoline)
- Smog Score: 5 (E85), 5 (gasoline)
- GHG Score: 4 (E85), 3 (gasoline)

Photo from Chrysler Group LLC

Dodge Grand Caravan

- 3.6L 6 cyl engine
- Starting MSRP: $20,995
- 12 mpg city, 18 mpg highway (E85)
- 17 mpg city, 25 mpg highway (gasoline)
- Smog Score: 6 (E85), 6 (gasoline)
- GHG Score: 4 (E85), 4 (gasoline)

Dodge Journey

- 3.6L 6 cyl engine
- Starting MSRP: $24,495
- 13 mpg city, 18 mpg highway (E85)
- 17 mpg city, 25 mpg highway (gasoline)
- Smog Score: 6 (E85), 6 (gasoline)
- GHG Score: 4 (E85), 4 (gasoline)

Ford E-150/E-250

- 4.6L 8 cyl engine
- Starting MSRP: $28,760
- 10 mpg city, 18 mpg highway (E85)
- 13 mpg city, 17 mpg highway (gasoline)
- Smog Score: 2 (E85), 2 (gasoline)
- GHG Score: 1 (E85), 1 (gasoline)

Ford E-150/E-250

- 5.4L 8 cyl engine
- Starting MSRP: $29,780
- 9 mpg city, 12 mpg highway (E85)
- 12 mpg city, 16 mpg highway (gasoline)
- Smog Score: 2 (E85), 2 (gasoline)
- GHG Score: 1 (E85), 1 (gasoline)

Ford E-350

- 5.4L 8 cyl engine
- Starting MSRP: $31,740
- Fuel economy data not available
- Smog Score: 2 (E85), 2 (gasoline)
- GHG Score: Not available

Photo from Ford Motor Co.

Ford Escape FWD/4WD

- 3.0L 6 cyl engine
- Starting MSRP: $24,670
- 13 mpg city, 17 mpg highway (E85)
- 18 mpg city, 23 mpg highway (gasoline)
- Smog Score: 6 (E85), 6 (gasoline)
- GHG Score: 5 (E85), 4 (gasoline)

Photo from Ford Motor Co.

Ford Expedition 2WD/4WD

- 5.4L 8 cyl engine
- Starting MSRP: $37,370
- 10 mpg city, 15 mpg highway (E85)
- 14 mpg city, 20 mpg highway (gasoline)
- Smog Score: 6 (E85), 6 (gasoline)
- GHG Score: 2 (E85), 1 (gasoline)

Ford F-150

- 3.7L 6 cyl engine
- Starting MSRP: $22,790
- 12 mpg city, 17 mpg highway (E85)
- 17 mpg city, 23 mpg highway (gasoline)
- Smog Score: 6 (E85), 6 (gasoline)
- GHG Score: 4 (E85), 3 (gasoline)

Ford F-150

- 5.0L 8 cyl engine
- Starting MSRP: $24,986
- 11 mpg city, 15 mpg highway (E85)
- 15 mpg city, 21 mpg highway (gasoline)
- Smog Score: 6 (E85), 6 (gasoline)
- GHG Score: 3 (E85), 2 (gasoline)

Photo from Ford Motor Co.

E15 and Intermediate Blends

EPA has approved the use of ethanol-gasoline blends up to E15 for use in all MY 2001 and newer vehicles. Fuel containing more than 15% ethanol is only approved for use in FFVs. This includes various intermediate blends now available from stations with ethanol blender pumps. Using blends higher than E15 in non-FFVs may result in maintenance, safety, or performance problems.

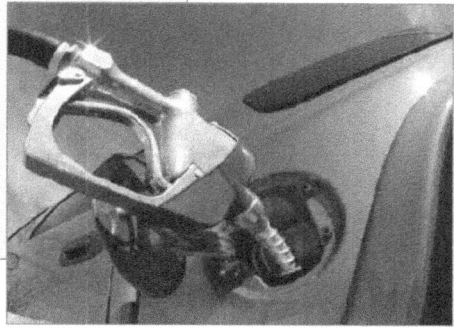

Photo from iStock/16015643

Ford Fusion

- 3.0L 6 cyl engine
- Starting MSRP: $24,670
- 14 mpg city, 21 mpg highway (E85)
- 20 mpg city, 28 mpg highway (gasoline)
- Smog Score: 5 (E85), 5 (gasoline)
- GHG Score: 5 (E85), 5 (gasoline)

Ford Police Interceptor FWD/AWD

- 3.5L 6 cyl engine
- Starting MSRP, fuel economy, and emissions data not available

Ford Police Interceptor FWD/AWD

- 3.7L 6 cyl engine
- Starting MSRP, fuel economy, and emissions data not available

Ford Super Duty F-250/F-350

- 6.2L 8 cyl engine
- Starting MSRP: $29,225
- Smog Score: 2 (E85), 2 (gasoline)
- Fuel economy and GHG data not available

GMC Terrain FWD/AWD

- 2.4L 4 cyl engine
- Starting MSRP: $24,500
- 15 mpg city, 22 mpg highway (E85)
- 22 mpg city, 32 mpg highway (gasoline)
- Smog Score: 6 (E85), 6 (gasoline)
- GHG Score: 6 (E85), 6 (gasoline)

Photo from General Motors

GMC Terrain FWD/AWD

- 3.0L 6 cyl engine
- Starting MSRP: $26,300
- 12 mpg city, 18 mpg highway (E85)
- 17 mpg city, 24 mpg highway (gasoline)
- Smog Score: 6 (E85), 6 (gasoline)
- GHG Score: 4 (E85), 3 (gasoline)

GMC Yukon Denali/Denali XL 2WD/4WD

- 6.2L 8 cyl engine
- Starting MSRP: $53,560
- 10 mpg city, 14 mpg highway (E85)
- 14 mpg city, 18 mpg highway (gasoline)
- Smog Score: 5 (E85), 5 (gasoline)
- GHG Score: 2 (E85), 1 (gasoline)

Jeep® Grand Cherokee

- 3.6L 6 cyl engine
- Starting MSRP: $26,995
- 13 mpg city, 17 mpg highway (E85)
- 17 mpg city, 23 mpg highway (gasoline)
- Smog Score: 5 (E85), 5 (gasoline)
- GHG Score: 4 (E85), 3 (gasoline)

Photo from Chrysler Group LLC

Lincoln Navigator 2WD/4WD

- 5.4L 8 cyl engine
- Starting MSRP: $57,665
- 10 mpg city, 15 mpg highway (E85)
- 14 mpg city, 20 mpg highway (gasoline)
- Smog Score: 6 (E85), 6 (gasoline)
- GHG Score: 2 (E85), 1 (gasoline)

Photo from Ford Motor Co.

Mercedes-Benz C300 4MATIC

- 3.0L 6 cyl engine
- Starting MSRP: $38,020
- 13 mpg city, 18 mpg highway (E85)
- 18 mpg city, 25 mpg highway (gasoline)
- Smog Score: 5 (E85), 3 (gasoline)
- GHG Score: 4 (E85), 4 (gasoline)

Photo from Mercedes-Benz USA

Nissan Armada 2WD/4WD

- 5.6L 8 cyl engine
- Starting MSRP: $38,490
- 9 mpg city, 13 mpg highway (E85, 2WD)
- 12 mpg city, 19 mpg highway (gasoline, 2WD)
- Smog Score: 5 (E85), 5 (gasoline)
- GHG Score: 1 (E85), 1 (gasoline)

©2011 Nissan

Offset Your Costs

A transition to alternative fuels or advanced vehicles usually entails upfront costs. But in many cases, such expenditures can be offset by lower operating costs and by federal and state tax exemptions, rebates, grants, or other incentives. Visit *www.afdc.energy.gov/afdc/laws* to browse and search a database of laws and incentives related to alternative fuels and vehicles, air quality, fuel efficiency, and other transportation topics. Be sure to consult with your tax advisor to determine your eligibility for any incentive.

See page 19 to find out how to calculate the long-term costs of vehicle ownership.

Photo from iStock/16749919

Nissan Titan 2WD/4WD

- 5.6L 8 cyl engine
- Starting MSRP: $27,410
- 9 mpg city, 13 mpg highway (E85, 2WD)
- 13 mpg city, 18 mpg highway (gasoline, 2WD)
- Smog Score: 5 (E85), 5 (gasoline)
- GHG Score: 1 (E85), 1 (gasoline)

Ram 1500

- 4.7L 8 cyl engine
- Starting MSRP: $21,475
- 10 mpg city, 12 mpg highway (E85)
- 14 mpg city, 19 mpg highway (gasoline)
- Smog Score: 6 (E85), 6 (gasoline)
- GHG Score: 1 (E85), 1 (gasoline)

Toyota Sequoia 4WD

- 5.7L 8 cyl engine
- Starting MSRP: $44,780
- 9 mpg city, 12 mpg highway (E85)
- 12 mpg city, 17 mpg highway (gasoline)
- Smog Score: 5 (E85), 5 (gasoline)
- GHG Score: 1 (E85), 1 (gasoline)

Toyota Tundra 4WD

- 5.7L 8 cyl engine
- Starting MSRP: $31,215
- 10 mpg city, 13 mpg highway (E85)
- 13 mpg city, 17 mpg highway (gasoline)
- Smog Score: 5 (E85), 5 (gasoline)
- GHG Score: 1 (E85), 1 (gasoline)

Photo from Toyota Motor Corp.

Volkswagen Routan

- 3.6L 6 cyl engine
- Starting MSRP: $27,020
- 12 mpg city, 18 mpg highway (E85)
- 17 mpg city, 25 mpg highway (gasoline)
- Smog Score: 6 (E85), 6 (gasoline)
- GHG Score: 4 (E85), 4 (gasoline)

Photo from Volkswagen Group of America

Biodiesel

Ford Super Duty F-250/ F-350/F-450

- 6.7L 8 cyl engine
- Starting MSRP: $36,900
- Fuel economy and emissions data not available

Super Duty F-350. *Photo from Ford Motor Co.*

Biodiesel is a renewable option for diesel vehicles.

Biodiesel is a clean, renewable fuel produced from a wide range of vegetable oils and animal fats. B100 is pure biodiesel, but consumers typically buy biodiesel blends ranging from B5 (5% biodiesel, 95% diesel fuel) to B20 (20% biodiesel, 80% diesel fuel). B20 has been shown to perform well in diesel vehicles, even in cold weather and in older engines. All manufacturers have approved B5 for use in all diesel engines.

Vehicles currently approved by their manufacturers for B20 use are listed below.

- Chevrolet Silverado 2500/3500 HD Pickups and Express 2500/3500 Vans, equipped with the 6.6L V-8 Duramax Turbo Diesel
- GMC Sierra 2500/3500 HD Pickups and Savana 2500/3500 Vans, equipped with the 6.6L V-8 Duramax Turbo Diesel
- Ford Super Duty F-250, F-350, and F-450, equipped with the 6.7L V-8 Power-stroke Turbo Diesel
- Ram 2500/3500 HD Pickups, equipped with the 6.7L V-8 Cummins High Output Turbo Diesel (fleet calibration only).

Biodiesel is different from straight vegetable oil.

To make biodiesel, producers filter and process vegetable oils or animal fats to remove water and contaminants. The fats and oils are then mixed with alcohol and a catalyst to produce biodiesel. B100 must be produced to strict specifications (ASTM D6751) to ensure proper performance of any blend level. Straight vegetable oil is not a legal motor fuel, and its use can void vehicle warranties.

Biodiesel is good for the environment.

The use of biodiesel blends in place of conventional diesel can reduce tailpipe emissions, such as particulate matter and hydrocarbons. Relative to conventional diesel fuel, biodiesel derived from soybeans reduces overall life cycle emissions of carbon dioxide by more than half.

U.S. Department of Energy

Clean Cities advances the nation's economic, environmental, and energy security by supporting local actions to reduce petroleum use in transportation. A national network of nearly 100 Clean Cities coalitions brings together stakeholders in the public and private sectors to deploy alternative and renewable fuels, idle-reduction measures, fuel economy improvements, and emerging transportation technologies.

For more information, visit:

- *www.cleancities.energy.gov*
- *www.fueleconomy.gov*
- *www.afdc.energy.gov*

www.ingramcontent.com/pod-product-compliance
Lightning Source LLC
Chambersburg PA
CBHW071344310526
45790CB00018B/1354